My Year of Design 2GO

A Daily Journey of Thinking and Making

for Quilters and other

published by Quilt around th

My Year of Design 2GO
A Daily Journey of Thinking and Making
for Quilters and other Textile Lovers

Jutta Hufnagel

published by Quilt around the World GmbH

© 2017 Quilt around the World GmbH

Quilt around the World GmbH
Gross-Nabas-Str. 3
D-81827 Muenchen
Germany
www.quilt-around-the-world.com

Content and layout: Jutta Hufnagel

Editors: Anke B. Calzada, Derry Godden, Johann Gutauer, Jutta Hufnagel

Art Work: Quilt around the World GmbH

© 2017
Herstellung und Verlag: BoD – Books on Demand, Norderstedt.
ISBN: 978-3-7431-1238-4

Printed in Germany

Preface

My Year of Design - our very personal journey of thinking and making - started in 2014 with weekly online design exercises for the readers of the online portal Quilt around the World. As its popularity has been increasing steadily, My Year of Design (MYoD) continues online, in print and in the shape of exhibitions in Germany and other countries.

The idea for this workbook came while reading the comments of a MYoD1 participant. She is a very busy mother of three, very active in her community and supports her husband in running the family business. Elisabeth wrote that she carried the MYoD1 exercises wherever she went - to her children's football training, to a doctor's appointment, simply everyhwere.

We kept this book small and light-weight so that you, too, can carry it wherever you go. It fits easily into every handbag!

We hope that the exercises will inspire you to think in new directions, to perceive your surroundings in new ways and to translate your ideas, your sketches and your notes into wonderful and unique textile pieces - no matter whether you are an art quilter or a craft quilter!

Whatever you make from these exercises - we would love you to keep in contact with us and to show us your work! The more pieces we can showcase in our MYoD online gallery, the more interesting it will be for everybody!

Have fun while thinking and making!

Jutta Hufnagel

Contents

> You should never have so much to do
> that you don't have enough time to think anymore.
>
> *Georg Christoph Lichtenberg*

Thank You!

I would like to extend my sincere thanks to...

... **Anke**, **Derry** and **Johann**, for supporting the MYoD idea from the very start and for constructive proofreading.

... all the contributors of previous MYoD editions who sent pictures of their wonderful work for the gallery and for the past exhibitions. **Your work and your feedback have always been a huge joy and an immense source of inspiration for me.**

... **Elisabeth Kriegenhofer,** who provided a part of the inspiration which led to the concept for this book.

... all friends and supporters who generously helped to make this publication possible.

Working with this Book

This book contains short design exercises which encourage you to leave well-trodden paths and **develop new ideas** based on **what you see, hear, feel and experience in your daily lives**. Some of the exercises are suitable for any situation or surroundings, others were created for specific situations, e.g. waiting for the bus or for your friend in a restaurant, watching your children playing sports, at the supermarket etc.

The exercises are independent of each other. You can do them in any order. We recommend that you get a rough overview first.

For your work with the exercises you only need this workbook and a pencil. A set of coloured pencils could also be helpful. The exercise is always printed on the upper page of a double page turned in landscape format. **The empty part of each double page is reserved for sketches, drawings and notes.**

It is not necessary to "finish" an exercise in one go. Revisit the exercises from time to time, add sketches, drawings and notes. Leave room to develop your ideas further and repeat the same exercise two or three times, always playing with different surroundings, emotions and situations.

If you think that you need more space than the one empty page, simply cut regular printing paper to the right size and place the sheets wherever you need them.

We would like to encourage you to draw as much as possible yourself instead of just taking pictures with your smartphone. First of all, there is the risk of drowning your "on the road" pictures in the hundreds and thousands of pictures in your phone's memory. Secondly, drawing is not just another method of documentation. In most cases, drawing will take more time and is more subjective and already an expression of your personal "designer's handwriting". By drawing, you will develop a much more intimate relationship with your motif.

Don't tell yourself or others that you can't draw. You might not be Michelangelo, but nobody expects museum-worthy drawings from you. Even Michelangelo had to practice his craft before he became an artist. **Almost all of us can walk, just as we can speak. We might never become prima-ballerinas, but we are able to set one foot in front of the other.**

When working on the exercises, there is **no "right" or "wrong"**. Follow your own path and have as much fun as possible. Nobody is looking over your shoulder to criticize you. Should you need support, feel free to contact us (contact information on page 104).

Enjoy the journey!

Jutta

The Exercises

Movements

e.g. at the children's sport practice or at any sports event

Observe what happens on the pitch or in the gym. It is not important which sport you are watching, whether your children are practicing their first steps or whether you have accompanied a confirmed sports fan to a match without being overly interested yourself.

What are the players doing, how and where are they moving? How many players/referees/assistants are on the pitch? Do they all have the same importance? Are they performing the same movements or are there differences?

Try to express the movements with curved lines. If you like, draw rectangles for the players - if there are different types of players, you could fill the rectangles with different textures, patterns or colours.

Translate your sketch into a textile piece.

Which techniques and materials would you choose to express movement? In what ways can you show the different types of movements and aspects such as direction and speed?

The existence of movement implies necessarily a body which is moved and a force which moves it.

Nikola Tesla

Three Lines, Two Circles and a Square

anywhere

Design a patchwork block or a small quilt which can be drawn with three lines, two circles and a square. Here are the "rules":

- First draw a square which represents the outline of your block or quilt. If you like, leave room for more than one block design.

- Draw a line from top to bottom. The other two lines should start on one side, but should not reach the other side.

- Draw two circles which touch the ends of the "loose" lines.

- Draw the square into your design in such a way that it touches or intersects at least two of the other elements.

How many different block or quilt variations can you think of?

You will find a similar exercise in the very first book of the My Year of Design series. For more information on all MYoD publications and activities, please go to page 100.

> A round man cannot be expected to fit in a square hole right away. He must have time to modify his shape.
>
> *Mark Twain*

Landscape of Sounds

anywhere

Close your eyes and listen to the sounds which surround you.

Is there background noise? Can you hear music, laughing (or crying) children, noisy machinery, screeching car brakes, twittering birds?

Try to identify as many sounds as possible. No matter where you are, you should be able to "collect" at least five different sounds.

Now think of ways to portray these sounds.

How would you draw inoffensive background sounds and loud and clattering noise in your acoustic foreground?

In what way could you translate "soft" and "agreeable" sounds? What would aggressive city noise look like in a sketch or drawing?

In a textile piece, you could use different portrayals of a landscape of sounds. Think about layering from back to front, a horizontal or vertical strip layout or an almost coincidental arrangement of your individual sounds.

Return to this exercise from time to time. There are so many landscapes of sounds that you could probably play an entire year with this exercise!

Tones sound and roar and storm about me until I have set them down in notes.

Ludwig van Beethoven

Budding Green

in the open air

When in the spring nature slowly reawakens from its winter slumber, plants start budding in the most diverse shades of green. If you look closely, you can discern yellow-green, green-green, brown-green, grass-green, spinach-green and probably a thousand more variations.

Take your coloured pencils and, on the next page, create a catalogue of green shades. Use as few pencils as possible and try to "mix" the different green nuances, e.g. with the help of hatching, the close placement of points and/or lines etc.

If you don't have coloured pencils with you, you could try to describe the colours with words. Once back home, use your descriptions to imitate the colours with water colours or coloured pencils.

Which shades of green do you like best? Which might you consider for your next textile piece? In what way could you translate mixed colours?

Should you come across this exercise during another season of the year - no problem! Make a catalogue of yellows for summer, red-orange for autumn and blue-grey for winter!

Grey, dear friend, is all theory
and green life's golden tree.

Johann Wolfgang von Goethe

The Salt and Pepper Still Life

in a restaurant or a bar

If you are waiting for a friend to join you, select three objects from your table and use them to create a still life.

The objects should differ in size and form. If possible, look for objects with varied surfaces/textures (e.g. rough versus shiny). Arrange and rearrange the objects until you are satisfied with your layout.

Sketch your final version on the next page. Reduce complexity and go back to the basic geometric forms.

Could this be the starting point for a textile piece? Do you have any ideas for the background of your still life? Will you leave it in its actual environment or will you create an entirely new background?

Life is not a still life.

Oskar Kokoschka

Not Only Nature has Texture

anywhere

The texture of a surface describes what it feels like or would feel like.

Look for as many different textures as possible. Look around you and document the different surfaces which surround you, e.g. the bark of a tree, a mirror, a paved street, your cat's fur, leaves from different trees, rusty hoarding etc. Use the next page and create a "catalogue of textures". Describe the textures with words and drawings. Write down where you found this texture and how you could find it again, if needed.

Of course you don't have to fill this page all at once. Come back whenever you have found another interesting texture.

When the page is full, study all your textures. Which surface is the most intriguing? What would you do to translate this texture into a textile piece?

Nature hates reason.

Oscar Wilde

Tense and Impatient

e. g. before a doctor's appointment or at a station/an airport with travel nerves

Depending on one's general attitude, one can sit calmly in a waiting room and see what transpires. However, one can be tense and impatient or even feel a perhaps irrational fear. Many people would give a lot not to have to enter their dentist's practice at all. Outwardly positive undertakings such as a holiday trip can lead to tense situations, e. g. when suffering from travel nerves or when delays endanger a connecting flight etc.

If, for whatever reason, you are feeling tense and impatient right now, listen to your inner self and try to express on the next page what you are feeling, e. g. with words or, even better, with a small sketch or drawing.

Which shapes lend themselves to express a feeling of stress or impatience? In what way will these shapes change when an element of fear is introduced? Which colours would you choose to portray stress, impatience and fear? Which format would you choose for your work?

Impatience, the mother of folly, praises brevity.

Leonardo da Vinci

Loops and Scrolls

anywhere

Draw, without pausing, five loops and then extend the line towards the opposite side of the page with one or more swinging scrolls.

Draw as many loops and scrolls as fit onto the page. Vary the position of the loops and change the character of the scrolls. Turn the book so that your loops and scrolls are angled differently.

Which loop/scroll variation do you like best? Does it have the potential to become part of a textile piece? Could it perhaps be a free-motion quilting pattern or has an interesting pattern emerged from the entire book page?

Consider transferring the resulting pattern onto textiles, e.g. with the help of various printing techniques or with fabric pens. Embroidery stitches lend themselves beautifully to portray lines. A length of wool/specialty yarn laid out in loops and scrolls can be fixed to a piece of carrier fabric by means of dry felting.

We want to prevent everything that is embellishment and ornateness. And embellishment is everything that is neither letter nor punctuation.

Friedrich Schiller

Cappuccino & Co

in a coffeehouse

Are you sitting in a coffee house waiting for your date? Why don't you order a cappuccino and enjoy it with all your senses. Make a few notes on the next page for every step.

- First of all, rejoice over the creamy milk foam crest and perhaps the cocoa powder pattern which the barista put on your cappuccino. Spend a little time observing how the cocoa powder slowly sinks into the milk foam.

- Close your eyes and let the smell of coffee take effect on you. Not only the smell from your cup, but also the smell of freshly ground coffee so typical of coffeehouses.

- Put a few sugar crumbs on your tongue, close your eyes and catch your first associations for "sweet".

- Sweeten your cappuccino if that is what you usually do and take a sip. Again close your eyes and catch the first associations.

Put aside your notes. Very possibly your date has arrived by now. Look at your notes a few days later and think about ways to use your "tastebud associations" in a textile piece.

> What makes the coffee sweet,
> the sugar or the stirring?
>
> *Jewish proverb*

Posters

almost anywhere, especially in towns

Search for posters and large size advertisements.

At first, just look at them without concentrating too much on the content. Then analyse which elements were used in the design of the poster. Document your analysis on the next page.

- Which colours, which shades, tints and tones do you see?

- In what way did the designer use lines and shapes? Include the shapes created by text areas and, when in doubt, reduce them to rectangles, squares etc.

- What role does the focus of the poster play? Is there strong contrast or rather a more subtle approach?

Based on your analysis, decide whether you like the poster or not. Do you think that the composition conveys the content well, the so-called "message"?

Now think about ways to create your own variation of the poster in a textile piece. Is the content of the poster important for your design?

If you are interested in design and composition, our online course MYoD3 could be for you. More information on page 101.

All art is composition - that is the key to everything.

Pierre Bonnard

Snippet of the Day

anywhere, especially on holiday

Rethink the day, how you spent it, what happened. Do you have any piece (of paper) which belongs to your day? E.g. a train ticket, a receipt from a shop, a parking ticket, perhaps even a newspaper clipping, a recipe, a newspaper advertisement?

Glue the snippet of the day onto the next page and make it the centre and the theme of a textile design. Don't think too long about what you could do, just throw yourself into it and start drawing and creating.

What is developing?

> Wisdom is not only in the years,
> but in the head.
>
> *Kurt Tucholsky*

Fast, Faster, Fastest

anywhere

Observe the people around you and the different speeds they move at.

Turn the next page to portrait format. Concentrate on one person and draw a zigzag line with lots of peaks if the person is moving fast or with few peaks if the person is moving more slowly.

If you like, you could also interrupt the lines when the person stops moving. When the movement pattern changes, curved and wavy lines could also be useful. The thickness of the lines could be adapted according to your own criteria etc.

When the next page is filled with zigzag lines, put the exercise aside for a few days. Take it up again and think about ways to translate your "Fast, Faster, Fastest" into a textile piece.

Consider using a completely different base material, such as jute, leather, felt etc.

All life has no standstill
and the most beautiful is the fastest.

Johann Jakob Wilhelm Heinse

Still Life with Pineapple

at a vegetable market

Go to a market or to a supermarket and buy a (ripe) pineapple, some apricots and a piece of root ginger. Or some other pieces of fruit and vegetables.

Play around with the fruit and create several different still lives. Make rough sketches and concentrate on the basic shapes.

Decide on the variation which you like best. What could a textile version of your still life look like?

Note: In your textile translation take into account the texture of the different fruit!

Pineapples, apricots and ginger root make a wonderful jam. In this case you need a really ripe pineapple and ca. double its weight in ripe apricots.

Under the Clouds

anywhere

Observe the sky on cloudy days.

What about the colours of the clouds? Find at least one colour in each cloud besides white.

This exercise becomes much more interesting if you take it up on several days at different times. Storm clouds can also be very exciting. While observing a (thunder)storm, be sure to take the necessary safety measures!

Look closely at each cloud shape and note or sketch the structures.

Are there any interesting patterns which could be further developed in a textile piece?

The cloud never comes from the quarter of the horizon from which we watch for it.

Elizabeth Gaskell

Same Old, Same Old

at train stations, at bus or tram stops

Timetables are surely among the most boring reading matter on earth. They can also become quite annoying, mostly when one notices that one has just missed the desired mode of transport and the next is not due for hours.

Should you ever be in this situation, use the timetable to search for possible sources of inspiration:

- Take a few steps back and concentrate on the rhythm of the lines and columns.

- Study the stops. Are there places or streets which you don't know? Imagine what the surroundings there might look like (WITHOUT using the Internet!).

- Count the number of connections per day. Design a patchwork block with exactly this number of pieces.

Small stations are proud,
that express trains must go past them.

Karl Kraus

Hot Sand

at the beach

If you are lying on a beach right now, this exercise is just perfect for you. Lie on your towel, preferably, directly on the ground.

Close your eyes and concentrate on what your body is feeling. Are you lying on hot sand or perhaps on pebbles? What comes to mind? How do you sense the heat and the sunbeams on your skin? Or are you lying underneath an umbrella?

Let some sand or pebbles run through your fingers. What are you sensing? Which associations are created by the sand? In what ways could you incorporate these feelings in a textile piece?

Now concentrate on the smells which surround you. Are you smelling salt? Your sun lotion? Smells of food from a nearby beach bar? Smells which you can't identify?

Document your impressions with words and ideally also with a few sketches. Make sure that you note down the place and the date and perhaps staple a photo of the beach to this page later on.

What could be the textile outcome of your notes and drawings?

The exercise on page 12 on Landscapes of Sounds is also very suitable for a day at the beach!

If one does not know to which port one is sailing, no wind is favourable.

Seneca

Boooring...

anywhere

My Year of Design 2GO is meant to make the daily, sometimes boring, "in-between times" a little more amusing. For this exercise it is necessary, however, to be a little bored to begin with.

What does this boredom feel like?

Close your eyes and imagine that you are trying to portray your feeling of boredom with horizontal bars. What could interrupt the different bars of boredom? What colours are appropriate? Which colours would you choose if somebody said that you could not use grey?

Are there different shades of your boredom? In what way could they be expressed?

... boring is the one who has a few old thoughts which he has afresh every day.

Marie von Ebner-Eschenbach

The Car Make Bingo

at the kerbside, e. g. at a bus stop

Are you waiting somewhere at the kerbside? E.g. for the next bus? Use the waiting time and observe the cars going past.

Choose three popular car makes and assign them the (patchwork) shapes below. Count and document how many cars of each make pass.

Later, on the bus or at home, design a patchwork block with the exact number of shapes.

Note: Always remember that you don't necessarily have to design a pieced block. You could always appliqué the shapes!

Square:

Triangle:

Circle:

Failure is simply the opportunity to begin again, this time more intelligently.

Henry Ford

The Loudspeaker Mystery .

at a train station or an airport or wherever there are loudspeaker messages

Most loudspeaker messages are a waste of time because the sound quality is so bad that you can't understand anything anyway. Loudspeakers whoosh, the surrounding architecture creates impressive reverberations and the crowds drown the rest in the background noise they are making.

Again, use this fact to your designer's advantage.

Think about ways to translate the cut up sentences, the cracks and whooshing sounds, the reverberations and the human mumbling into a textile piece.

What overlays what? In what ways could you express disruption and the technical cracks and whooshing sounds?

Only travelling is life, as vice versa life is travelling.

Jean Paul

The World Behind a Windshield Wiper

in the car as front passenger

Have you ever consciously observed how raindrops hit the windscreen of a moving or idling car, how they disperse and how they are "extinguished" time and time again by the windscreen wiper?

Concentrate for a few minutes on the interaction of raindrops and windscreen wiper. Of course only if you are not the driver!

What patterns emerge?

How does the world change behind the windscreen? What elapses, what is distorted?

Even more intriguing are the patterns which emerge when the raindrops are allowed to disperse when the car is idling. Watch how they disperse and mix and document what you have seen.

In what ways could the "dance of the raindrops on the windscreen" be translated into a textile piece?

Everybody complains about the wheather, but nobody does anything against it.

Mark Twain

I Don't Speak Outlandish

in a foreign country where people speak a different language

Should you currently be in a foreign country and ideally not speak the language, why don't you try this exercise?

Look around and look for a word of which you don't know the meaning. Do NOT try to research its meaning at this point!

Note down the word on the next page.

Then ponder the word for a while. What could be its meaning? Is it something beautiful? Something menacing? What colour is it? Is it moving? Does it have paws? Or hooves? Or more than two eyes?

Let your imagination run riot and then make a sketch on the next page.

In what ways could you put the result into a textile piece?

Once you consider your design finished, go and research the real meaning of the word. Which do you like better, the "correct" translation or your own interpretation?

Should you have no immediate plans to travel to a country with a different language, leaf through a foreign-language magazine. Or ask a friend, who speaks a foreign language, to lend you a book to look for a suitable word.

Languages are the archives of history.

Ralph Waldo Emerson

Light, Light, Light

in a restaurant, in a bar - ideally after dark

Look around and analyse the different light sources in your surroundings.

How is the room illuminated in general? Are there any individual light sources, e.g. above the bar, with candles on individual tables or from reflecting surfaces?

Are the lights all the same colour?

Make some notes and sketch the respective "areas of light" on the next page.

Then observe the faces surrounding you. What effect do the different lights have on the shadows on the faces and perhaps also on the skin and hair colour? Do glasses, jewellery and clothes reflect a part of the light?

In what ways could you translate this light/shadow/colour scene in a textile piece?

Note: It might be advisable here to abstract what you have observed.

A similar exercise can be found in the book My Year of Design TWO. For more information on the MYoD publications, please go to page 100.

Art is unlike football.
Sometimes you score most
when you are in an offside position.

Edgar Degas

Portrait of Somebody Unknown

in the train, on the bus, in the aeroplane

Look unobtrusively for a person in your surroundings and draw his or her portrait on the next page.

Only use basic geometric shapes - ovals, circles, squares, rectangles, triangles etc.

Then consider what you find most striking in that person's face. Have you captured this element with the shapes?

What is your model feeling right now? Try to express whatever you think he or she is feeling with the help of coloured pencils.

Could you use this portrait in a textile piece?

Note: Make sure that your model doesn't feel disturbed by ostentatious staring on your part. Of course you can always explain what your intentions are and ask the person's permission. Since your portrait will remain very abstract, you will not have to worry about violating personal rights!

Every human being carries some magic in the face; and there is somebody who likes this.

Christian Friedrich Hebbel

The Wind, the Heavenly Friend

anywhere in windy weather

Look around or through the window and watch how the wind is changing the landscape.

If you cannot hear or feel the wind, what would tell you that it is blowing? Why do you think the wind is blowing fiercely or more moderately? How do living creatures adjust to windy weather?

On the next page, create a very simple landscape with three or four horizontal lines. Then sketch at least three plants, two different animals (two- or four-legged) and an object, all of which are influenced by the wind.

Whether the wind is blowing in the same direction and with the same force, is up to you. It would be good practice, too, if you drew the same landscape several times setting a certain wind situation each time which would then influence all the figures.

In what ways could you translate the wind-afflicted or the wind-elated figures in a textile piece?

The wise man speaks prudently,
the fool with certainty about the coming weather.

Wilhelm Busch

Secret Code on the Street

in the passenger seat of the car

Note down three to five number plates, ideally from different states or countries.

Contemplate the letter and number combinations for a few minutes. What are your first associations? Can you form words or sentences? Is it possible to combine these words or sentences derived from all number plates to a (very short) story?

In what ways could you translate this story in a textile piece?

If making up a story seems too complicated:

Try to change and modify the numbers and letters collected while working on this exercise into an absurd, but attractive "jumble of symbols". Consider changing the size, the font, the colour of the letters and the numbers.

How could you use this "jumble of symbols" in your work? Could you for example create a stencil, a printing block or a silkscreen?

If you can, leave the petty
and search for the great.

Gottfried Keller

As Long as it is Chocolate

anywhere

Eat a piece of chocolate. Close your eyes, enjoy the taste and pay attention to your first thoughts.

If you like, do this exercise with several pieces of chocolate. In this case, make sure that you have different kinds, e. g. with nuts, raisins, chili etc.

What will your very special chocolate quilt look like?

What would it look like if you didn't use any browns?

Taste is nothing else
but the ability to form an own opinion
on what the masses like or dislike.

Jean-Jacques Rousseau

Rows of Windows

in the city

Walk through your town or city and contemplate the rows of windows of the multi-storey (office) buildings you see while wandering the streets.

Could you use the different "grids" in a textile piece? Think beyond the layout of a quilt! What happens if you super-impose several of the "office building grids"?

All architecture aims at influencing the mind, not only at protecting the body.

John Ruskin

Happy Anticipation

e. g. in a concert hall or in the cinema before the performance/film starts

On page 20, we have already worked with a tense kind of impatience.

Here we chose the more agreeable counterpart, anticipation and happy expectation of a longed-for event.

Look within yourself and think about your anticipation and your expectation of a beautiful and perhaps stimulating evening. In what way could you use these feelings in your design work?

Try to abstract your feelings as much as possible and, if possible, make them independent of the actual event. Make a quick sketch as long as the impression is still fresh.

After the performance, contemplate your design in peace and quiet. Were your expectations met?

Note: For later it is surely interesting to know when and for which event you made your "snapshot of feelings". We recommend that you note down the date and the name of the performance, too.

> You have to do your own growing
> no matter how tall your grandfather was.
>
> *Abraham Lincoln*

Dancing in the Rain

anywhere in rainy weather

Next time when you are walking, either for pleasure or running some errands, don't open your umbrella immediately when the first drops of rain start falling. Stop for a moment, let your head fall backwards, close your eyes and let a few raindrops fall onto your face.

What are you feeling? Do you see any images behind your closed eyelids? What is going through your head?

Document your first assocations and make a few sketches in preparation for later use in a textile piece.

If you are really weather-proof, repeat this exercise - perhaps only just in your mind - when the weather is really bad, i.e. when the wind literally drives the rain into your face.

By the way: This exercise also works very well with snowflakes!

*O man, learn to dance,
or else the angels in heaven will not know what to do with you.*

St. Augustine

Wiping

anywhere

To some extent, we see My Year of Design as a counter-movement to the modern ways of killing time or of filling the days to the brim with "productive" activities. Therefore, this book very decidedly was not published as an e-book, but quite old-fashionedly printed on paper.

Nevertheless, you are asked to do some wiping on the next page - as if the surface were a smartphone!

First, rub a little of the lead from your pencil onto the paper. If you have coloured pencils with you, add some coloured pigment, too. If you are very daring, you could also experiment with spice powders.

Make some wiping movements with your index finger. You could wet your finger a little and/or exert more or less pressure.

What is the result?

Could you develop your wiping picture into a textile piece?

Not what we have but what we enjoy,
constitues our abundance.

Epicurus

Repetitions

anywhere

Look around and search for structures which consist of repetitions, e. g. accumulation of points, lines, shapes, forms, patterns, colours etc.

Analyse the structures and reflect why you like or dislike them.

Use your favourite as the basis for a textile design.

Thoughts without content are empty,
intuitions without concepts are blind.

Immanuel Kant

Reducing Animals

at the zoo or on a farm

Observe the animals at the zoo or on a farm.

What is the most characteristic trait of each animal?

Can you express this characteristic with only one design element (e. g. point, line, shape, colour, pattern)?

If you put your design into a textile piece, will the original motif still be recognizable?

Talent hits a target no one else can hit.
Genius hits a target no one else can see.

Arthur Schopenhauer

Wandering Colour Charts

anywhere

We all subject ourselves more or less to the dictates of fashion when we choose our clothes. At least most of us do. Depending on individual taste, more or less successful colour combinations are the outcome.

Observe the people around you, e. g. on the bus or in the train going to work. Note at least five colour combinations which you like, and five colour combinations which you consider unsuccessful.

Could these colour combinations form the basis for a textile piece?

You could also focus on bags and backpacks. Or, when you are on the beach or at a lake, use the bathing suits and towels as starting points.

There is no blue without yellow and without orange.

Vincent van Gogh

The World Passes by

on the train

When you look out of the window of a train, the world is passing by at breakneck speed. If you are looking ahead, it races towards you, if you are looking backwards, it appears as if the world is flying away from you.

In what ways could you portray this movement and speed in a textile piece? Consider three views: looking ahead, looking out sideways and looking backwards.

How does the view change the way you deal with movement and speed?

All the world is stage,
and all men and women merely players.

William Shakespeare

Rather a Third Than a Quarter

anywhere

Choose any object from your surroundings and observe and analyse it in detail.

On the next page, draw a very light line parallel to the right hand edge and one third in.

Make a rough sketch of the selected object which lies exactly on your marked line. You can draw the object close to its reality or you can abstract it.

Put aside the exercise for a few days. Then take it up again and design the areas left and right of your object so that the outcome is harmonious and could be used as the starting point for a textile piece.

I paint the things as I think them, not as I see them.

Pablo Picasso

The Colour of the Aura

anywhere

Imagine that every person's aura has a certain colour. Look around and observe, as unobtrusively as possible, the people around you. Decide on a colour for each person.

For each observed person, draw a small coloured square on the next page. If you don't have enough different coloured pencils, mix colours with the help of hatching.

Put aside the exercise for a few days. Then take it up again and identify "new" colour combinations which you have not used before.

In what ways could you use these colour combinations in your next textile piece?

Experience teaches us that the individual colours produce special moods.

Johann Wolfgang von Goethe

Fresh Vegetables

at a market or in a supermarket

Contemplate the wares on a vegetable stand at a market or go to the fruit and vegetable department of a supermarket.

Make a sketch of the presentation of goods and don't be stingy with the colours. Reduce the fruit and vegetables to simple shapes, but draw as many individual pieces as possible. Work with colour shading and pay attention to the contrast between the fruit.

If you don't have that much time, you could always just fill one area and complement your drawing whenever you are more at leisure.

Are you developing any ideas for a project? Which techniques could you use to put your fruit and vegetables into textiles? Always consider appliqué, any dyeing and printing techniques, and the use of non-textile objects, such as buttons and beads.

Every era has its challenge,
and by solving it mankind is progressing.

Heinrich Heine

Self-Portrait

anywhere

In previous exercises we have dealt with portraits of other people several times. Now is the moment of truth - we will create a self-portrait!

When you are on the road, you probably don't have a mirror with you. Here you are asked to make a self-portrait "from within".

Ask yourself who you really are. How do you see yourself, how do you think others see you? Are you a happy person? Do you have the tendency to brood? Do you have occasional bursts of fury? Is it easy to make you laugh or cry?

Think about yourself and then create a design which puts your thoughts into shape and colour.

If this soul-searching is too much for you right now, simply contemplate your mood of the day and try to put it on paper and perhaps later into fabrics.

Nobody knows themselves.

Francisco de Goya

Slanting Grid

anywhere

Draw four straight but not quite vertical lines and two straight but not exactly horizontal lines on the next page. The lines should go right to the edges of the book.

Choose a simple patchwork block and draw it in each of the sections. Colour your "slanting quilt".

What is evolving?

No wisdom can combat a foolishness which is the current fashion.

Theodor Fontane

Contrasts

anywhere

Look around and search for strong contrasts. Note down and document at least five different objects which contrast well with their environment or which carry strong contrasts within themselves.

Note also how the contrast is formed.

Put aside this exercise for a few days. Take it up again and analyse your list. Have you collected a broad range of contrasts or are they very similar (e. g. only light/dark or only colour contrasts)?

When the contrasts are very similar, choose a different type of contrast and focus on that for a while, continuing to collect examples.

Can you use this "new" contrast in a textile piece?

*Art does not portray the visible,
but art makes visible.*

Paul Klee

What Binds the World and Guides its Course

anywhere

Provided your state of health and your general fitness allow, balance on the kerb of a quiet street.

What is necessary to keep yourself and your life in balance? What does "life balance" really mean?

How can you create balance in a textile piece? In what ways can this term be contextualized?

Everything existing in the universe is the fruit of chance and necessity.

Democritus

Towards the Horizon

anywhere, especially out of doors in the country

Look towards the horizon.

How many "layers" can you discern from where you are standing to the horizon?

You should divide the landscape into at least three, but no more than five layers. Divide the next page into two more or less equal design areas and sketch this first set of "landscape layers" into one of them.

Change the scenery, e. g. continue your walk/travels to another place or simply wait a few days until you are in another environment anyway.

Repeat the exercise and sketch the new "landscape layers" into the second design area.

Can you combine the two landscapes? Could you perhaps mix the different layers in order to create a perhaps surreal new landscape?

What happens?

> We all live underneath the same sky,
> but we don't have the same horizon.
>
> *Konrad Adenauer*

Floors

anywhere

Floors are an excellent source of inspiration for quilters and textile lovers. Not only mosaic floors, but also simple tile patterns and parquets carry ideas for innumerable quilts.

Use the next page as your personal catalogue of floors. Return often to this exercise and add as many promising floors as possible.

When you have worked through this entire book, come back to your floors and choose one to work into a textile piece.

All that you have to do,
is to find the right key at the right time.

Johann Sebastian Bach

Look for the Interesting in the Mundane

in the car as passenger or at the bus station

Most engineers do not share the opinion that car lights are something mundane. However, in the context of today's traffic, the individual car light is certainly not of particular interest.

On the other hand, you can detect intriguing shapes while idly watching the passing traffic which is why you are asked to find at least five different car lights (front or back lights) and sketch them roughly on the next page.

In what ways could you use these shapes, all or just one or two, in a textile piece?

Who that can go to the source,
should not go to the jug.

Leonardo da Vinci

Splish, Splash

anywhere near water

Expressing water with textiles is not easy. You need to observe closely and be willing to experiment a lot, always running the risk that the result will not meet your expectations.

Look for places where you can observe water: at the sea, on a river bank or at a lake or simply on a bench in a park next to a fountain. Analyse the "colours" of water and the way light is reflected.

Then pick one aspect and think of ways to express it with textiles.

Water is not only a visual feast. Close your eyes when drinking and pay attention to the "stories" the water "tells" you. What are your first associations?

You will find lots of ideas about many aspects of water in textile surface design in Michaela Mosmüller's book "Water Variations". More information on page 103.

Water is the principle of all things,
and to water everything returns.

Thales of Milet

A Final Note

We hope that you have liked the **My Year of Design 2GO** exercises and that they have enlivened many grey and boring everyday situations.

Should this book have been your first encounter with **My Year of Design,** please go to page 100. Here we have listed and explained other My Year of Design publications and activities.

We, i.e. the entire team of Quilt around the World, would be very happy if you contacted us. Send us pictures of your sketches, textile experiments and finished work. On our website

www.quilt-around-the-world.com

My Year of Design is an active and very lively part, e.g. in the shape of online galleries which will also be created for My Year of Design 2GO.

Sources

We have taken the quotes either from literary works or have researched (and translated them) at these internet sites:

www.brainyquote.com
www.aphorismen.de
www.wikiquote.de
www.gutezitate.com

What comes Next?

More My Year of Design

My Year of Design

The first My Year of Design book is a collection of design exercises inviting you on a journey of thinking and making. This journey will lead you off the beaten paths of quiltmaking and will help you see the world around you with different eyes.

My Year of Design started as a weekly online series in 2014. On more than 140 pages, you will find over 60 completely revised exercises, thereof 5 bonus exercises previously unpublished, inspirational quotes of famous writers, painters, sculptors and other clever people, interviews with participants from around the world giving you insight into their approaches to their own design adventure, and a gallery showing pieces resulting from the online version of My Year of Design.

22,90 €
ISBN: 978-3-7392-0070-5

My Year of Design TWO

My Year of Design TWO is a collection of intriguing and unusual design exercises for quilters and textile lovers. All exercises follow a red thread through art history. In 18 chapters and one additional previously unpublished bonus chapter the design elements of different eras in art history are explored and used as basis for amusing and challenging design exercises.

As in the online edition, coincidence and mystery play important roles and are the basis for four self-contained exercise series.

22,90 €
ISBN: 978-3-7431-2676-3

My Year of Design THREE

My Year of Design THREE (MYoD3) is our third journey of thinking and making and offers a comprehensive online course in design for quilters and other textile crafters. Design is a language - a visual language which can help convey messages and which can help to create work which is visually and sensually pleasing.

MYoD3 continues the tradition of the previous MYoD publications in challenging you with playful, amusing and sometimes unexpected exercises. These exercises are accompanied by inspirational pictures, background information (you could call this "design theory" if you were so inclined) and feedback on the pieces you produce based on MYoD3.

MYoD3 is divided into three modules of six chapters each. Each month, you will receive a detailed feedback on at least one piece you have made based on the respective exercises.

You will need a PC with internet access and software to display PDF documents.

30,00 € (per module. Important: Limited number of participants!)

More information: www.quilt-around-the-world.com/en/MYoD3

49mysteries

Our popular Block Mysteries are back! 49mysteries brings you a new exciting and fun block riddle each week and the respective detailed sewing tutorial a week later – for a whole year!

Moreover, you will have access to the new Quilt around the World Academy tutorials which will support you in translating your own designs into fabric!

You will need a PC with internet access and software to display PDF documents.

25,00 €

More information: www.quilt-around-the-world.com/en/49mysteries

25connections

And for all fans of the Coincidental Connections we have a very special "web freebie" for you: Every other week, we publish the instructions for designing one of 25 blocks which you can make into an extraordinary quilt sampler in the course of a year.

Free!

More information: www.quilt-around-the-world.com/en/25connections

Order the books via your book shops, via your favourite quilt shop or directly via our website:

www.quilt-around-the-world.com

When ordering from our webshop, please take into account that, as a very small company, we cannot compete with the "big players" neither regarding delivery times nor fees for packing and postage. In return, we donate 1 € for every copy sold directly from our webshop or during quilt events to Doctors without Borders.

Books by Other Authors

Water Variations
Inspiration for Textile Surfaces
Michaela Mosmüller

This book is dedicated to the textile translations of different aspects of the element water. Detailed step-by-step tutorials offer an exciting and entertaining approach to textile surface design for beginners. At the same time, advanced quilters find lots of inspiration for their own experiments in the unusual and unconventional techniques.

22,90 €
ISBN: 978-3-7431-2678-7

Wort und Faden - Word and Thread
Heidemarie Mönkemeyer

With the help of fabrics, lace and edgings - old, stashed and left behind - the textile artist Heidemarie Mönkemeyer tells the forgotten stories of women who lived long ago and commemorates them in word and thread.

This personal artist portrait gives you a comprehensive insight into the works of Heidemarie Mönkemeyer. The 35 pieces show the development of her textile pictures and the accompanying texts and poems since 2008.

18,00 €
ISBN: 978-3-7412-2234-4

About Quilt around the World

Quilt around the World is an innovative, interactive and international online portal for patchwork and quilting.

Our online and book publications aside, we organise international quilt activities such as block swaps and challenges. Should you be interested in our work, please visit our website at:

www.quilt-around-the-world.com

or e-mail us at:

info@quilt-around-the-world.com

Sneak Preview

4th International Block Swap

Start date: 1 May 2017

All information at www.quilt-around-the-world.com

Friends and Supporters

Should you need material and/or support in the realization of your designs, you can contact the following shops:

Quilt und Textilkunst
Christine Köhne
Sebastiansplatz 4
80331 Munich
Germany

Telephone: +49-(0)89-23077401
www.quiltundtextilkunst.de
info@quiltundtextilkunst.de

Quilthouse Purgstall
Angelika Steinböck
Kirchenstraße 26
3251 Purgstall an der Erlauf
Austria

Telephone: +43-(0)7489-30164
www.quilthouse.at
quilthouse@gmx.at